Unearthing
The Lost Words
of JESUS

Unearthing
The Lost Words
of JESUS

The Discovery and Text of
The Gospel of Thomas

JOHN DART and RAY RIEGERT

COMMENTARY
John Dominic Crossan

Seastone

BERKELEY, CALIFORNIA

Published by: Seastone, an imprint of Ulysses Press
P.O. Box 3440
Berkeley, CA 94703-3440

Library of Congress Cataloging-in-Publication Data

Dart, John, 1936–
    Unearthing the lost words of Jesus : the discovery and text of
    the Gospel of Thomas / authors John Dart, Ray Riegert ;
    introduction by John Dominic Crossan.
            p.   cm.
    Includes bibliographical references.
    ISBN 1-56975-095-5
    1. Nag Hammadi codices.   II, 2.   2. Manuscripts, Coptic--
Egypt--Cairo.   3. Gospel of Thomas--Criticism, interpretation, etc.
I. Riegert, Ray, 1947–   .   II. Gospel of Thomas.   English.
III. Title.
BS2860.T52D37   1998
229'.8--dc21   98-4422
                                                                 CIP

ISBN: 1-56975-095-5

Printed in the USA by R.R. Donnelley & Sons

10 9 8 7 6 5 4 3 2 1

Book Design: Sarah Levin, Leslie Henriques
Editorial and production staff: Steven Zah Schwartz, David Wells,
    Aaron Newey
Cover photograph: The Image Bank/Guido Alberto Rossi
Insert photographs: Photographs of Muhammed Ali, cliff face of Jabal al-Tarif,
    and The Gospel of Thomas courtesy of Bastiaan Van Elderen. All remaining
    photographs courtesy of the Institute for Antiquity and Christianity in
    Claremont, California.

Distributed in the United States by Publishers Group West, in Canada by Raincoast Books, and in Great Britain and Europe by World Leisure Marketing.

Table of Contents

PART ONE

The Discovery

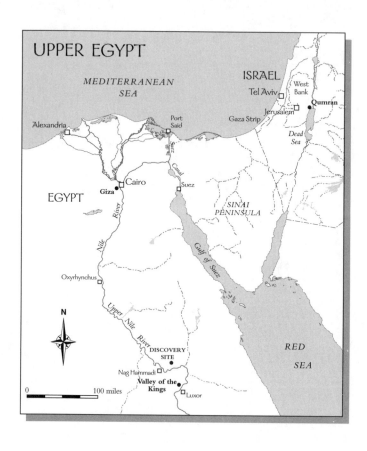

CHAPTER ONE

Blood Feud

DECEMBER ALONG THE UPPER NILE RIVER IS THE IDEAL time to dig for *sabakh*. The devastating summer heat is gone and the valley soil more pliable than it is in the dry season. December 1945 was particularly auspicious. World War II had ended four months before. Egypt was enjoying a welcome hiatus between the ravages of Rommel and the coming war over the new state of Israel. A rare peace had descended upon the Middle East.

But the camel drivers digging in the sloping base of a cliff near the river had a personal war to worry over. There were seven of them, including Muhammed Ali and two of his brothers. The area where they hunted the nitrate-rich fertilizer, not far from their native village, appears to the unknowing eye safe and unassuming. Located three hundred miles south of Cairo, it is a spot where the Nile flows from east to west. The small village of Nag Hammadi lies near a bend in the river just a few miles away.

It is here that a railroad track marked a borderline as menacing to Muhammed Ali and his band as the line in the sand that had separated German tanks from the forces of the Allies. South of the tracks, inside the river bend, was the territory of Ali's clan. To the north lay Hamrah Dum, the fortified village of a warring clan that had already killed Ali's father. The seven *sabakh* diggers were in a no-man's land between the secure embrace of their village and a region of certain death. The Hawwaris of Hamrah Dum claimed to be a noble race of Arabs descended from the Prophet himself. One thing about them was certain: They hated Ali's people with a blood passion.

Ali's brother was the one who discovered the jar. Abu al-Majd, a lad of fifteen, was working with the older men along a level area near the talus slope that angled up toward a honeycombed cliff. Abu was picking in the soil beneath a barrel-shaped boulder when he unearthed a large reddish-hued urn. It was two feet high and had four small handles at the top. The mouth was covered by a bowl and sealed with bitumen.

Muhammed Ali immediately took charge. At first the older brother—though a seasoned man of twenty-six—was too frightened to break open the mysterious container. It was the type of vessel that might contain a jinn, an evil spirit that could appear in human or animal form and exercise supernatural powers over people. But greed eventually overcame fear. Ali reasoned that, more likely than the dark home a demon, the clay jar could be full of gold. He raised his mattock and smashed it.

Thirty years later Muhammed Ali still feared that spot. It was September 1975 when an American scholar finally caught up with the elusive villager. Ali's mattock had revealed something far more astounding than a jinn, and this tall, angular professor wanted to unravel the mystery surrounding the discovery. Though the site was within five miles of Ali's village, the Egyptian had not returned to it for three decades.

James M. Robinson was a singularly determined man with an intense demeanor and a slight Southern drawl. He had graduated with honors from the Columbia Theological Seminary around the time Ali was wielding his digging tool. Now he had found the man whose discovery had determined his academic career.

But Ali was adamant. Even after revealing a scar above his heart inflicted by a rival clan member and boasting that he would kill his assailant, Ali refused to lead Robinson back along the Nile River. Robinson tried bribery and eventually challenged the villager's courage before Ali relented.

Even then Ali's conditions were like something out of a Keystone Cops comedy. He would be dressed in American clothes and sit next to Robinson in the back of a Russian-made jeep. In case of gunfire, Robinson would serve as shield: on the way out, the scholar would sit on the side nearest Hamrah Dum, then for the ride back, Ali would switch seats with him so that Robinson would always be positioned between the Egyptian and the rival village. The day chosen was during the Islamic month of Ramadan, a period of fasting. To further ensure his safety, Ali suggested they go during the late afternoon when hunger and thirst would keep his enemies indoors. The driver was to ride past the cliffs without stopping. Ali would point out the place of discovery.

As the party drove along the rockface Ali directed them to a tomb. Robinson later returned, without the nervous camel driver, and excavated the site for five days, coming up with nothing. Another guided search would be necessary. This time Ali stepped from the car, marched forward without hesitation to the barrel-shaped boulder and began digging in the earth, proclaiming it the spot. He told of how his camel had been tethered on the south side of the boulder and recalled that all seven men had been afraid the rock would collapse on them.

Describing the scene years later, Ali admitted it was an image of gold that finally drove him to smash the jar. When the ancient ceramic shattered, it seemed for a moment that his dream was fulfilled: tiny yellow flakes filled the air. The Egyptian villager had either conjured an amber-colored jinn or struck it rich.

In fact, what he found was priceless. Muhammed Ali, an illiterate field hand who would never afterward be able to remember exactly when the event occurred, had made one of the greatest archaeological discoveries of the twentieth century. Those gilded flecks were actually tiny fragments of papyrus; Ali's treasure was a collection of thirteen books containing over fifty ancient manuscripts, many of them Christian, dating to the fourth century.

Among them was *The Gospel of Thomas*, a collection of over one hundred sayings of Jesus purportedly written down by the "doubting Thomas." Historians had long known about the gospel from references in the writings of early church fathers, but in almost two thousand years a complete copy had never been located. While some of the sayings could be found in the New Testament, many were unique. They portrayed Jesus as a wise man, Zen-like at times. In the years that followed, biblical scholars would claim that some of them were closer to the historical Jesus than the New Testament itself.

One person's trash, as they say, is another's treasure. Muhammed Ali was a very disappointed man. What the world called a precious historical discovery, the villager saw as pottery shards and a stack of old leather-bound scraps of papyrus. He began tearing the ancient codices apart, intent on sharing them with the other men. Perhaps fearing Ali, and considering his offer insincere, the others refused to take them. So Ali unwound his turban, spread out the headdress and stacked the books inside. Swinging the load over one shoulder, he unhobbled his camel and headed back home. There, in the room where he housed his animals and feed, Ali dumped the load.

During the next decade, as experts and government officials alike began realizing that this humble camel driver's cache was the largest collection of unknown apocryphal Christian writings ever found, antiquities dealers would offer them on the open market from Cairo to New York, and the question of access to "the Nag Hammadi library" would flare into an international struggle ultimately involving the United Nations. That night Ali's mother, in search of kindling for her outdoor clay oven, cast some of them into the fire.

Later the family tried to sell the books, hoping to pick up a few Egyptian pounds. No one was buying. They bartered a few for oranges and cigarettes. Various accounts also mention them receiving a little tea and a supply of sugar. At some point Ali learned the documents were written in Coptic, an ancient language used by Christians in Egypt.

This meant they probably belonged to the church, which could be trouble for Ali. Possession of such antiquities was a crime, and Muhammed Ali was already being watched by the authorities. In fact, the police were searching his house every night for weapons. It had been less than a year since his father, a night watchman, had killed an intruder who turned out unfortunately to be from the village of Hamrah Dum. Within hours Ali's father was murdered, shot through the head and dumped next to the body of the man he had killed. Ali's mother overcame her grief long enough to instruct her seven sons to keep their mattocks sharpened. This was the situation when Muhammed Ali unearthed the manuscripts.

About one month later the fears of the police were realized. Someone ran to the Ali home to tell them their father's murderer had fallen asleep nearby—he lay along a dirt road, a jug of sugarcane molasses by his side. James Robinson recounted the horrendous scene after interviewing Muhammed Ali: "The sons grabbed their mattocks, fell on the hapless person before he could flee, hacked him up, cut open his heart, and dividing it among them, ate it raw, the ultimate act of blood vengeance."

CHAPTER TWO

The Frenchman in the Museum

WITH HIS BROODING EYEBROWS AND THIN MUSTACHE, Jean Doresse cut a striking profile. His thick dark hair, sharply parted to one side, lay combed in a long sweep that lent a maturity and elegance to his boyish face. He was a thirty-year-old graduate student when he and his wife arrived in Cairo in September 1947.

Doresse had spent the previous years studying and lecturing in Paris, steeping himself in the history of early Christianity in Egypt. Now the French Institute of Archaeology in Cairo had invited him to spend three months exploring for Christian remains in a region three hundred miles south of the city. Well trained in the language and culture of the area, Doresse was exhilarated with the prospect of visiting ancient monasteries that were the oldest in Christendom.

Christianity had put down some of its earliest roots in Egypt. Long before the Muslims arrived in the seventh century, Christian monks under St. Pachomius launched a building campaign that developed countless monasteries and convents along the Upper Nile and Red Sea. Several were located along the northern shores of the bend in the Nile River that ends at Nag Hammadi.

At first local conditions frustrated Jean Doresse's plan to visit the monasteries. A cholera epidemic swept through Egypt during autumn 1947. Within a month it had killed five thousand people, primarily in the Nile delta. Government health measures forced the eager Parisian to postpone his trip to Upper Egypt. In any case, the delay would give him time to explore Old Cairo, the most ancient part of the city and a neighborhood strongly linked to Christianity in Egypt. Here a town had grown up in the sixth century B.C. around a fortress that guarded the canal between the Nile and the Red Sea. Legend has it that a nearby church rests where Jesus' parents took him when they fled from King Herod. Other stories place St. Mark here in 45 A.D., founding the first Christian church in Egypt and making his first convert, a Jewish shoemaker from Alexandria.

The Frenchman wandered through the ancient quarter, past a huddle of dark churches. This, he realized, was the center of Coptic Christianity. During the early years of the religion, as Rome and Constantinople became the capitals of the Catholic and Eastern Orthodox churches, a different brand of Christianity developed here. Today over six million people, fully ten percent of Egypt's population, are Coptic Orthodox Christians. They share a national culture with their Muslim compatriots but maintain a separate spiritual identity. Some claim that the crosses they wear around the neck or tattooed on their wrists, similar in design to Egyptian *ankhs*, represent the first crosses. Others point out that the Bible was translated into Coptic, the local language of the time, *before* it appeared in Latin.

Doresse walked along cobbled streets that lay in the shadows of twin circular towers, past a water gate constructed in the days when the Nile River lapped at the foundation of the old fortress, past the Hanging Church with its marble pulpit and ivory altars. He saw high-walled houses and medieval churches flanked by cemeteries. But there was a method to the Frenchman's meandering. He was going to meet Togo Mina.

A dark-complexioned man of forty-one, Mina stood about five feet five inches, with slightly stooped shoulders that only emphasized the difference in height between him and six-foot tall Doresse. The two men were only about a decade apart in age, but Mina, who suffered from diabetes and other ailments, appeared much older. He had known the Frenchman's wife Marianne years before in Paris when they were studying at the École des Hautes Études and had even proposed marriage to her.

Now the former suitor was director of the Coptic Museum, a major repository of relics from the Coptic period in Egyptian history. Jean Doresse, who had studied Egyptology at the same academy two years later, knew of Mina's scholarly reputation from his wife and professors at the school. Before leaving Marseilles in September, "I wrote and received the most friendly answer," Doresse later recalled. "He was anxious to see me, but he would not write why."

Doresse entered a contemporary yellow stucco structure that contrasted sharply with the antique buildings and Roman ruins of Old Cairo. He passed through an enclosed courtyard that displayed marble columns and statues. The museum's two wings, with their carved ceilings and stained glass domes, enclosed peaceful gardens.

Mina wasted no time revealing why he was so interested in Doresse's visit. "He opened a drawer of his desk, took out a voluminous packet, and showed me, in a book cover of soft leather, some pages of papyrus filled with large fine Coptic writing." Mina suggested the documents might date from the third or fourth century. Then he asked Doresse if he could identify the contents of the papyrus pages.

After reading only "the first few words," the Frenchman realized the text had been written by an ancient Christian sect, the Gnostics. He knew that by the fourth century the Gnostics—who saw Jesus more as a spiritual guide than the Messiah and believed self-knowledge led to godliness—were under attack by mainstream Christians.

Only later did Doresse cast his eyes on *The Gospel of Thomas*; that first day he saw a manuscript entitled *The Gospel of the Egyptians*, which spoke of the "Father whose name cannot be uttered." The neatly written, ragged-edged text went on to speak of the "powers" and "lights" of the heavens. Another text, attributed to the disciple John, described an appearance by Jesus after his resurrection.

Doresse warmly congratulated Mina on the extraordinary discovery. Where, he asked the official, had this amazing find been made?

CHAPTER THREE

Hamrah Dum

He had purchased the texts, Mina told Doresse, the year before the Frenchman arrived. Someone had shown them to a member of the museum's board who had an interest in Coptic, and he had sent the man on to Togo Mina. Since then, Mina continued, he had located other manuscripts, held by a Belgian antiquities dealer named Albert Eid. Eid had a shop in a section of the city called Khan Khalil. Would Doresse be interested in seeing them?

The Frenchman responded eagerly, and the two men jumped into Mina's car, Mina switching to the dark-tinted sunglasses he always wore when driving. "Eid was good enough to let me look at the manuscripts he had bought," Doresse recalled. In appearance and content they resembled the museum's papyri, though the pages were in poorer condition.

Mina and Doresse departed the shop determined to find out where the two sets of manuscripts had been discovered. Perhaps there were more to be found at the source. But inquiries along the antiquities grapevine yielded little. "They spoke mysteriously of a large find of manuscripts having been made near a hamlet called Hamrah Dum, well to the north of Luxor," Doresse said.

The two men returned to Eid's shop, and Mina told the dealer that the Coptic Museum wanted to buy the manuscripts. Then he warned the Belgian not to take the documents out of Egypt. Eid said he understood. Just to be sure, they made him agree to supply photographs of the fragile papyrus leaves to Doresse. If the pages left the country or mysteriously disappeared, the photos would be handed over to the museum at no cost.

Eid further tantalized them. There was a possibility, he said, that still more codices (the leather-bond papyrus "books") could be found in Cairo. He was unclear of where they were or who held them, however. So Mina concluded, according to Doresse, "that it was one more legend of fabulous discoveries aimed at increasing the price of Eid's codex."

Still, there *was* that rumor about a find at Hamrah Dum. The place, coincidentally, was located in the very area Doresse had been headed when he first arrived in Egypt. Railway service remained suspended because of the cholera epidemic, but the Frenchman could fly to Upper Egypt. His tour of the monasteries, once a reward for years of study in Paris, was about to become a mere cover story disguising Doresse's true mission.

He rambled around the Coptic ruins of the Upper Nile and explored the remains of Egypt's earlier greatness, the monuments of the pharaohs, all the while hoping to hear stories of a large papyrus discovery. Inquiring openly could drive up the price of any codices still circulating. "The silence that invariably hides the real circumstances surrounding great finds, and which we had thought we might break," he said, "was again impenetrable."

Unknown to Doresse, or to the rest of the world, the significance of another historic discovery was coming to light in Jerusalem. The Dead Sea Scrolls, discovered by Bedouin tribesmen about a year before in caves around Qumran, were identified by an Israeli archaeologist as priceless antiquities at the same time Doresse was poking around Hamrah Dum.

The Frenchman failed to find any more manuscripts. His trip to the Luxor region a bust, and his three-month assignment nearly at an end, Doresse returned to Cairo in December 1947. "Togo Mina was now definitely persuaded that there was nothing more to be discovered," he said. Cairo newspapers reported the museum's acquisition the following month, but "it caused no great stir in a country so inured to archaeological marvels." Back in Paris, Doresse collaborated with his professor on a report for the scholarly world that aroused a "moderate" degree of interest. *Le Monde*, the leading newspaper in Paris, gave it three sentences.

Just a few months later, Doresse received a packet in the mail from Cairo filled with photographs of more unknown papyrus texts. He appealed for travel funds from the academy and by October 1948 was on his way back to the Middle East. The photos had come from a woman named Maria Dattari, the daughter of a noted coin collector. She was, she claimed, the owner of the manuscripts. Together with her "business manager," an antiquities dealer from Cyprus named Phocian J. Tano, she invited Doresse to inspect the cache. Doresse had actually met Tano the year prior, just before leaving Egypt. Hinting that there were more documents around the city, the dealer had urged him to stay. As it turned out, the Cypriot was working through a man named Bahij Ali, a questionable character known as "the one-eyed outlaw." Through a series of shrewd maneuvers and a trip out to the discovery area, Tano had bought up most of the manuscripts.

When he scanned the Dattari-Tano codices, Doresse found himself gazing at hundreds of papyrus pages held together in the now-familiar soft leather bindings. The magnitude of the collection was overwhelming. He ran his eyes and fingers over four times as many texts as he had previously seen. Most were treasures never before available to historians. In all, Tano had eight codices and parts of four others.

"I went from surprise to astonishment," Doresse recalled, encountering "sensationally attractive titles." There was *The Letter of Peter to Philip*, purportedly written by Saint Peter himself, as well as *The Revelation of Adam to His Son Seth*, in which the first man describes how God created him. And in this pile was *The Gospel of Thomas*. Doresse began reading a text that would become known as "the fifth Gospel." Among the sayings it contained were many unknown to Matthew, Mark, Luke and John. "These are the secret words," it recorded, "that the living Jesus spoke."

Doresse saw very few of those secret words, or of the other manuscripts either. "I was allowed to make no more than a rapid inspection of them," he recalled. Maria Dattari and Phocian Tano guarded their possession jealously. Punctuating their suspicions were the air raid signals, which blared at what seemed to Doresse the slightest provocation, announcing that Egypt was at war with Israel and cutting short the few evenings he was permitted to peruse the manuscripts.

CHAPTER FOUR

Smuggling the Sacred

WAR IN THE MIDDLE EAST—IGNITED BY THE CREATION of Israel the year before—was only one of the problems confronting Mina and Doresse when they began the delicate matter of negotiating for the Dattari-Tano collection. Complicating the situation was the Egyptian government, which liked to confiscate historical treasures instead of paying a fair price. The practice forced antiquities owners to go underground, slipping goods out of the country and selling them on the black market.

Despite these difficulties, the museum director secured a promise of government funds. It was a major coup; overcoming war and government chicanery, Mina had set the stage for one of the most important antiquities purchases of the century. The Coptic Museum would possess the only complete collection of sayings by Jesus ever found.

But Mina's coup could not match the political catastrophe that fell on December 28, 1948. That day a member of the radical Muslim Brotherhood assassinated the Egyptian prime minister, creating havoc in the capital. The Coptic Museum would have to wait for the formation of a new government.

While it waited, another set of ancient texts slipped from the museum's grasp. Albert Eid had once bragged to Mina and Doresse about plans to smuggle his manuscripts out of the country, past "completely inefficient" government agents. That winter he carried through on the boast. As he left the country, the Belgian showed the antiquities department an assortment of carved figures, coins and other items he intended to sell abroad—nothing the authorities would want to retain in Egypt. What he didn't show them, and what eluded their oversight, he was soon offering on the open market in the United States. Eid asked $20,000 from the University of Michigan library, an institution known for its papyrus collections, but they considered his price too steep. In New York, with *The Gospel of Truth* and other texts in hand, he approached the Paul Mellon-funded Bollingen Foundation, dropping his price to $12,000.

Frustrated by the foundation's refusal even to keep the manuscripts in its safe, he departed for Brussels, where he put his pages in a safety deposit box. By the next year, Eid was dead and, according to one authority, "It was not known where the codex was to be found."

Meanwhile, Maria Dattari was stopped at the Cairo airport while trying to remove her papyri from Egypt. She was headed for Rome, according to one report, to present the collection to the Pope! The Egyptian minister of education informed her she could not export the codices and offered to buy all eight for three hundred Egyptian pounds each. Dattari politely declined. The authorities seized the collection, telling the Italian woman and her business manager that Doresse would assay the collection. For a time it appeared the new government would pay them a fair price, fifty thousand Egyptian pounds perhaps. But on July 25, 1949 that regime also collapsed.

The next act in this melodrama seems drawn from the final scene of *Raiders of the Lost Ark*. In that movie, archaeologist-adventurer Indiana Jones has survived a pit filled with poisonous snakes, been dragged behind a Nazi army truck and escaped a supernatural firestorm. He has risked death and dismemberment to recover the Ark of the Covenant, the 4000-year-old sacred chest that Moses carried out of Egypt. Acting in patriotic fashion, Indiana presents his find to the U.S. Army. The government, instead of announcing this historic discovery to the world, crates up the Ark, assigns an inventory number and buries it deep within the bowels of a storage warehouse. As the final credits roll, it appears the Ark may rest unseen for several more millennia.

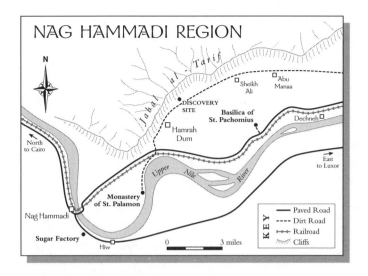

NAG HAMMADI REGION

N

Jabal al-Tarif

Sheikh Ali

Abu Manaa

DISCOVERY SITE

Basilica of St. Pachomius

Dechneh

Hamrah Dum

North to Cairo

Upper Nile River

East to Luxor

Monastery of St. Palamon

Nag Hammadi

Sugar Factory

Hiw

0   3 miles

KEY

——— Paved Road
- - - Dirt Road
‒•‒ Railroad
Cliffs

Change the crate to a piece of luggage, reduce the time lapse to seven years, and we are back to the story of *The Gospel of Thomas.* The book, together with the other parts of Muhammed Ali's discovery that had been confiscated by the Egyptian government, was packed away by the Department of Antiquities as "a temporary measure." In the ensuing years, Tano and Dattari fought a lengthy and futile legal battle to have the documents returned, only to see them ultimately declared national property. In the interim, most of the Nag Hammadi library, with its startling insights into the historical identity of Jesus and the nature of early Christianity, sat unopened in a suitcase from 1949 to 1956.

CHAPTER FIVE

The Jesus Curse

THE YEAR 1949 WAS PARTICULARLY HARD ON TOGO
Mina. The museum director was caught between international smugglers and a government that changed hands
more often than the documents he was pursuing. He was
simultaneously negotiating with shadowy antiquities dealers and unreliable officials while trying to keep the Nag
Hammadi library from being scattered all over the world.
This shuttle diplomacy was doomed to failure. Soon his
health collapsed as well. He was sick for several months and
then, because of conditions Doresse claimed were height-
ened by anguish and frustration, Mina died at the early age
of forty-three.

In Doresse's mind, it was a strange series of events: a
political assassination; the fall of the government; Mina's
demise; the disappearance of a set of manuscripts from
Europe; the sealing of a suitcase filled with priceless texts.
Was it, he wondered, simply greed and political instabil-

ity? Or could it also be the warnings in the gospels themselves that told of terrible consequences to "anyone gaining unlawful knowledge" of them.

Several of the works described themselves as "secret" and "hidden" mysteries. One, *The Secret Book of John*, actually contained a curse. The text is a dialogue between Jesus and his disciples. Near the end, Jesus tells John to write his teachings down and put them in a safe place. Then he cautions, "Anyone who exchanges these things for a gift, or for food and drink, or clothing, or for anything else, will be cursed."

Doresse knew that Upper Egypt, the site of the discovery, was also the scene of the pharaoh's curse. In 1922 archaeologists uncovered the 3000-year-old tomb of King Tutankhamen across the Nile River from Luxor. The burial chamber contained several secret compartments, each filled with gold and silver treasures. They also yielded a torrent of international publicity; and thousands of visitors were soon trekking through the Valley of the Kings every month.

During the next decade, more than twenty people reputedly connected with the unsealing of King Tut's tomb died. The first "victim" was the supervisor of the expedition, Lord Carnarvon, who succumbed in 1923 after a three-week illness caused by a mosquito bite. News reports began describing "the third victim," "the fourth victim" and so on. Some deaths appeared quite unusual, others were unremarkable, but talk of the curse persisted. Rumor told of an inscription that read, "Death will come swiftly to those who disturb the rest of the Pharaoh."

Egyptologists, pointing out that some "victims" were entirely unrelated to the tomb and having never found the inscription at the site, soon debunked the entire story. Since the Nag Hammadi-related deaths ended with Eid and Mina, the "curse of Jesus" also proved irrelevant. Of much greater interest to historians, and to Jean Doresse in particular, was the suggestion in *The Secret Book of John* to put the writings in a safe place. The advice had been well heeded; the papyri had rested undiscovered in the desert for centuries. But where? Had the library been hidden in a tomb, or within the walls of a monastery perhaps? And why? What were the circumstances surrounding its burial?

Archaeologists in Israel were asking similar questions about the Dead Sea Scrolls. A cave containing some of the scrolls was found sixteen miles east of Jerusalem in cliffs overlooking the Dead Sea. Nearby was Khirbet Qumran, Arabic for "the ruins of Qumran." By 1949 the site had been explored but systematic excavating not yet begun. Doresse, working on a find made two years before the scrolls, didn't even know yet the location of its source.

The discovery site remained cloudy but the political situation in Egypt was beginning to clear. In early 1950 the moderate Wafd party won a huge majority in the national election. Its leader, the new prime minister, was soon

Muhammed Ali, the discoverer of the Nag Hammadi Library, in front of a cave at Jabal al-Tarif.

Left: The cliff face of Jabal al-Tarif. The discovery of the Nag Hammadi codices was made somewhere in front of this promontory.

Below: Jabal al-Tarif cave inscription in Greek.

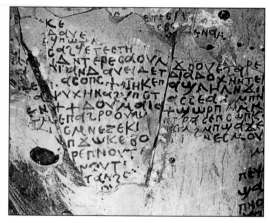

The Gospel of Thomas.

The Nag Hammadi Library.

Phocian J. Tano, the Cypriot
antiquities dealer.

Togo Mina (left) and Jean
Doresse study the Nag
Hammadi manuscripts at
the Coptic Museum.

Albert Eid, the Belgian antiquities dealer who took one of the manuscripts from Egypt to New York, then to Belgium.

driving through the streets of Cairo with Egypt's King Farouk to open the Parliament. Speaking from his throne, the rotund monarch pledged his country's loyalty to both the Arab people and the United Nations and promised to improve social conditions.

In this atmosphere Doresse left Cairo to find the answers that lay in Upper Egypt. If the papyrus books were found near Hamrah Dum, that would place the discovery site along the cliffs of Jabal al-Tarif, just a few miles east of the ruins of St. Pachomius' ancient monastery. Dressed in pith helmet, white scarf and sport coat, and accompanied by his wife Marianne, the Frenchman evoked the aura of a European adventurer. They worked their way along the eastern face of Jabal al-Tarif, feigning "deepest curiosity" in several caves that served as tombs for pharaohs from the Sixth Dynasty.

Pillagers had long since stripped the caves of relics, but in one grotto the explorers found the opening passages of Psalms 51 and 93 recorded on a wall, possibly the writings of a Christian monk. Greek invocations to Zeus appeared on another. Then the peasant guides who were leading the couple pointed out a strip of barren, sandy ground just below the caves. At the far end, Doresse reported, "they showed us a row of shapeless cavities." In one of these holes, the guides explained, local peasants digging for fertilizer had found a large jar filled with leaves of papyrus bound together like books.

It would be twenty-five years before the noted American professor James Robinson finally unraveled the history of this discovery, but the French graduate student was picking up the early threads. His guides told him a Coptic priest had been summoned from a nearby village to study the manuscripts. Doresse heard tales of laborers burning pages to heat their tea and selling their treasure for three Egyptian pounds to middlemen who offered it on the antiquities market in Cairo. He also learned the jar was found around 1945.

Now Doresse understood that local Egyptians had unearthed the library and when they had made their discovery, but the trail to the people who buried it in the first place was cold with the lapse of centuries. Using his knowledge of ancient Christianity and Egypt's early monasteries, Doresse began uncovering faint tracks that led back sixteen hundred years. He knew the Gnostics who compiled the library had eventually struggled with the region's mainstream Christians. Biographies of the monastery builder Pachomius, who died in 348 A.D., did not mention problems with Gnostics. But two decades after his death, St. Pachomius' successor, Theodorus, ordered that a letter listing the official books in the Bible be read in all the monasteries. The letter emphatically denounced heretical books like *The Gospel of Thomas*. Issued by Bishop Athanasius of Alexandria, one of the most famous figures in early Christianity, this was strong stuff.

It could have provided the opening monastery leaders had long sought to destroy all unorthodox books. Doresse theorized that Pachomius' follower was the same Theodorus who had once attacked a work, probably *The Secret Book of John,* as sinful and heretical. The Frenchman's reconstruction was only a possible scenario, but other evidence supports his ideas. Scraps of papyrus used to stiffen the covers of the books contained receipts dating from 333 to 348 A.D. This would place the binding of the books around 350 A.D. The crackdown came two decades later and the burial of the jar would have followed soon afterwards.

The gospels themselves are much older. Some scholars date parts of *The Gospel of Thomas* to the middle of the first century A.D., just a few decades after Jesus' crucifixion and *before* the writing of Matthew, Mark, Luke and John. Like the rest of the Nag Hammadi library, it was translated from Greek into Coptic. For Jean Doresse, who now had photographs of the lofty, rugged Jabal al-Tarif and the possible discovery site, the find was extraordinarily important, one of the most voluminous and precious libraries of papyrus writings ever found. As he explained in an article written for *Archaeology* magazine, "The number of codices, the care given to their binding and in particular the ancient techniques of these bindings, and the beauty of the different hands establish it as the most remarkable ancient library we possess."

The craftsmanship displayed in *Thomas* and the other "books" represented an entirely new genre. For centuries scribes had written on lengthy scrolls of papyrus like the ones found near the Dead Sea. But early Christians began developing the codex, a forerunner to the modern-day book, by cutting papyrus sheets into rectangles, punching holes along the side loose-leaf style, covering the manuscript with hide and binding it together with leather thongs. The leather covers from the Nag Hammadi library are among the oldest ever to survive.

CHAPTER SIX

Rabies and Revolution

ANXIOUS TO RETURN TO CAIRO AND PARIS TO SHARE what he now knew about the discovery, Jean Doresse inquired about a fast route back from Upper Egypt. Ever style conscious, he had driven out in a canvas-top Italian car custom built during World War II for one of Mussolini's generals and later captured by the British. But the route was long and circuitous, following the winding east bank of the Nile.

There was, he learned, a shorter route, one that led along the other side of the river. They would have to cross ten miles of flat desert at a point where the road ended, but it could be done. "We started after lunch without haste," he remembered. At a hamlet near the stretch of desert, they picked up a peasant guide who happily informed them their new route would lead to the ancient temple of the pharaohs at Dandara. The guide also promised the passage would be easy.

"Yes, it would have been easy with a camel," Doresse recalled, "but the man had no idea of the limited possibilities of a car. We started driving through something comparable to a bombed field for one hour before the petrol pump began leaking." Doresse would fix the pump, proceed a little farther, repair the pump again, move slowly forward again, and then work on the car once more, until darkness finally made it impossible to fix the leaks. Edging across the desert this way, the trail blazers eventually came within sight of the Dandara temple. At that point, "We left the car and proceeded on foot, with me running ahead of my wife and the so-called guide." On the way, he encountered a Bedouin village where a pack of dogs set upon him, drawing blood in several places.

A jerry-rigged fuel supply allowed the car to make it into camp, but Doresse now confronted a larger problem —rabies. It was impossible to have the dogs tested, so he returned immediately to Cairo to begin a month-long series of daily shots with "a medicine that looked like tepid butter." If the Frenchman connected the dog attack with the Jesus curse, he soon dismissed the notion when the rabies inoculations led to nothing more than a severe case of itching and actually provided an excuse to enjoy "the intellectual, artistic and gastronomical" delights of Cairo.

Progress on gaining access to the Nag Hammadi library moved with frustrating slowness during the next several years. Togo Mina was dead and Doresse watched helplessly as these remarkable manuscripts, buried for sixteen centuries, remained hidden from view. The suitcase containing *The Gospel of Thomas* and the rest of the Dattari-Tano collection was transferred from the Antiquities Department to the Coptic Museum in June 1952. Six weeks later, army officers led by Colonel Abdel Nasser staged a coup, overthrowing the monarchy and instituting a new regime. The Department of Antiquities, which had been under French direction since Napoleon's invasion of Egypt, was reorganized. The luggage would have to wait.

Finally in 1956, photographs of the pages of *Thomas* were published; the Egyptian government made a token payment to Tano for the confiscated manuscripts; and a committee was appointed to publish a standardized edition of the entire library. But in October of that year, an international dispute over the Suez Canal escalated into war. Israel, France and England invaded Egypt only to be turned back by political pressure from the United States and the Soviet Union. The committee would have to wait.

Long after the Suez crisis, the battle still raged over access to the manuscripts and the right to translate them. By then the struggle had escalated into an international dispute among scholars from the United States, Europe and the Middle East, forcing the intervention of UNESCO. But the United Nations' first act was to form a translation committee that never completed a single translation. *The Gospel of Thomas* was finally published in 1959, but as late as 1970, a quarter century after the discovery, only one-fifth of the rest of the Nag Hammadi library had been translated into English.

During this period, James Robinson, a member of the UNESCO committee, began exploring the Nag Hammadi countryside in the quest that eventually brought him face to face with Muhammed Ali. He also probed the Coptic Museum, asking to see manuscripts. Sorry, he was informed, they were under UNESCO control. He then turned to UNESCO, which claimed this was untrue. "In other words," he recalled, "I was getting the runaround."

The lanky Southerner was fighting for public access to the Nag Hammadi manuscripts. Through a contact in 1966 he obtained about seventy sheets filled with photographs of manuscript pages. Knowing he could only have them for a short period, "I spent three days and two nights in a dingy room transcribing the pages," he said. "I got so that I could do about four pages an hour." Later that year Robinson traveled to West Germany, where he stayed up all night copying another manuscript. "I was knocking myself out so I could come back to America with otherwise inaccessible texts."

Two years later, a UNESCO official in Paris surprised the professor by lending him the agency's Nag Hammadi photograph collection over a weekend. He gave Robinson half the documents as glossy prints and the rest as negatives. "No doubt," Robinson surmised, "so I could not abscond with a complete file of prints." The American found a photography shop willing to quickly develop 600 negatives. Meanwhile, Robinson laid the glossy prints out on the floor and "clicked away with my simple tourist camera." On Monday morning, a smiling scholar returned all the originals to the guileless official.

Through tact, stealth and persistence, Robinson eventually copied the entire library. It would be his name on the cover when *The Nag Hammadi Library*, the complete English translation, was finally published in 1977. For the last three decades, he has been director of the Institute for Antiquity and Christianity at Claremont Graduate University in California.

Jean Doresse's story did not end with such a flourish. When he returned to Europe in the early 1950s, he discovered that his status as a graduate student put him at a pronounced disadvantage among European scholars. His own professor isolated him from the French translation team and his collection of manuscript photographs mysteriously disappeared. Looking back years later, he understood that the Jesus curse was actually many curses which came, he realized, not in the form of death, but in the greed, jealousy and betrayal that had touched almost every one of the antiquities dealers, government officials and scholars who had ever had contact with the discovery of Muhammed Ali.

PART TWO

The Gospel of Thomas

OF THE MANY GOSPELS AND OTHER WRITINGS THAT Muhammed Ali unearthed near Nag Hammadi in 1945, the most remarkable was a collection of Jesus' sayings. It was a common practice in antiquity to gather together the wise remarks and spiritual utterances of a teacher. The books of Proverbs and Ecclesiastes in the Old Testament are part of this long tradition of wisdom literature. So it is not surprising that followers of Jesus combined over one hundred of his teachings into a book they called *The Gospel of Thomas*.

Historians have actually determined that Matthew and Luke used a similar document when they wrote their gospels. Beginning in the 19th century, they developed a theory that this sayings source must have existed since the authors of Matthew and Luke, who never met, used identical quotes of Jesus. This mysterious source became known as "the lost Gospel Q." Until the discovery of *Thomas* nothing similar had ever been located. The find lent strong support to the Q theory, particularly when scholars realized that over one third of the sayings in *Thomas* are similar to those probably contained in the Gospel Q.

Many mysteries surround both books. A central question of *The Gospel of Thomas* relates to the identity of the author. Though the book is attributed to the "doubting Thomas" of the New Testament, the real writer will probably never be known. Claiming a gospel was written by one of the disciples was a frequent technique used by early Christians to enhance the book's standing among other followers.

Most biblical scholars in the United States believe *Thomas* represents one of the many independent schools of Christianity that developed early in the history of the religion. Some date the original Greek version from which the Nag Hammadi Coptic document was translated as early as the second half of the first century, a few decades after the crucifixion. Such an early date could mean it was written before the New Testament gospels and is therefore closer to the source and more historically accurate. When the Jesus Seminar, an international group of biblical authorities, debated the reliability of various historical sources, they determined that of the nine New Testament parables thought to be stories actually told by Jesus, the *Thomas* version was closest to the original in six cases.

To specialists seeking a clear picture of the historical Jesus, the Nag Hammadi gospel demonstrates that early believers revered him primarily as a teacher of wisdom, not as an apocalyptic prophet or messiah. For the modern-day reader, this is the most important aspect of *The Gospel of Thomas.* It is a book filled with the wisdom of Jesus. Unlike the New Testament gospels, it contains nothing about his birth or death but presents him as a teacher, a wise man speaking directly to people about their lives. Jesus provides advice on getting along in the world and the importance of being true to ourselves. The message is strongly countercultural: he shuns materialism and directs the reader toward the simple life, a spiritual existence. There are parables about people who discover their true identity and immediately relinquish all their riches. He shows how they free themselves from the demands of a workaday existence to pursue what is truly important in their lives.

Jesus here is not the messiah but a social radical, telling listeners to reject society's phony piety and the hollow values of the business world. He promises that the reader has the potential of returning to "the light," a heavenly realm far removed from the earth. At times, Jesus sounds like a Zen master, particularly when he talks about the "kingdom of God" being right here, right now. Let the reader beware: this is not the Jesus taught in Sunday school and worshiped in glass cathedrals. In *The Gospel of Thomas* we meet Jesus before he was Christ, before the centuries of infighting and ecclesiastical embellishment that created today's semi-mythical figure. Here is Jesus as a sage, the personification of Wisdom, cast in the tradition of King Solomon or Buddha, a humble man with a powerful message.

THESE ARE THE SECRET WORDS that the living Jesus spoke and Didymus Judas Thomas wrote down.

1 WHOEVER FINDS the interpretation of these sayings will not taste death.

This saying, like the majority of the sayings in *The Gospel of Thomas*, begin with "Jesus said." To avoid redundancy, these introductory phrases have been eliminated.

2 LET WHOEVER SEEKS not cease from his seeking until he finds. When he finds, he will be troubled. When he is troubled, he will marvel and will reign over all.

IF THOSE WHO LEAD YOU SAY, "Look, the 3
kingdom is in heaven," then the birds of heaven will
precede you. If they say, "It is in the sea," then the
fish will precede you. Rather, the kingdom is within
you and outside you. When you know yourselves,
you will be known, and you will know you are
children of the living father. But if you do not know
yourselves, you live in poverty and you yourselves
are the poverty.

These words of wisdom are similar to the advice of Eastern
sages to "be here now."

THE PERSON ADVANCED IN DAYS will not 4
hesitate to ask an infant of seven days about the
place of life, and that person will live. For many
who are first will be last and they will become a
single one.

The theme of becoming one is common in ancient literature,
often referring to finding one's center and sometimes to sexual
intercourse.

5 RECOGNIZE what is in front of your face, and what is concealed will be revealed to you. For there is nothing hidden that will not be disclosed.

6 HIS DISCIPLES ASKED HIM, "Do you want us to fast? How shall we pray? Shall we give alms? What diet shall we keep?"

Jesus said, "Do not lie and do not do what you hate, because all things are revealed in the sight of heaven. For nothing is hidden that will not be revealed, and nothing is covered that will remain covered."

Saying 14 closely parallels this passage, answering each question the disciples ask.

Bₗₑₛₛₑ𝒹 ɪꜱ ᴛʜᴇ ʟɪᴏɴ that the man shall eat, so 7
that the lion will become human. Cursed is the
man whom the lion shall eat, and the lion will
become human.

Some scholars believe this saying is based on Plato, who said the soul was part human and part lion. It was the duty of the human part to tame its bestial side.

Hᴜᴍᴀɴᴋɪɴᴅ is like a wise fisherman who cast 8
his net into the sea. He drew it out of the sea full
of small fish. The wise fisherman found among
them a large, good fish. He threw all the small fish
back into the sea and chose the large fish without
hesitation. Whoever has ears to hear, let him hear.

This passage is similar to Matthew 13:47, in which the kingdom of heaven is compared to the net and the fish are likened to souls that are saved.

9   THE SOWER WENT OUT, filled his hand and
sowed. Some seeds fell on the road; birds came and
gathered them up. Others fell on the rock and did
not take root in the earth and did not produce.
Others fell among thorns; the thorns choked the
seeds and worms ate them. But others fell on good
ground and brought forth good fruit. These yielded
sixty per measure and one hundred and twenty
measures.

10   I HAVE CAST FIRE on the world and, look, I am
guarding it until it blazes.

The "fire" may refer to Jesus' teachings.

THIS HEAVEN WILL PASS AWAY and that which is above it will pass away. The dead are not alive and the living will not die. In the days when you ate what is dead, you made it alive. When you come into the light, what will you do? On the day when you were one, you became two. But when you have become two, what will you do?

This saying promises a third heaven as the ultimate goal, to be reached after "this heaven" and "that which is above it" disappear. The quote is also interesting because it sounds very similar to the passage in Mark and Matthew in which Jesus explains that "heaven and earth will pass away, but my words will not pass away."

THE DISCIPLES SAID TO JESUS, "We know you will go away from us. Who will be our leader?"

Jesus said, "Wherever you are, go to James the Just; heaven and earth came into being for him."

James was the brother of Jesus and head of the Jerusalem church. He became a major figure in the development of Christianity during the decades immediately following the crucifixion.

13   JESUS SAID TO HIS DISCIPLES, "Compare me to someone and tell me whom I am like."

Simon Peter said to him, "You are like a righteous angel."

Matthew said to him, "You are like a wise philosopher."

Thomas said to him, "Master, my mouth is incapable of saying whom you are like."

Jesus said, "I am not your master. Because you drank, you are drunk from the bubbling spring that I measured out."

And he took Thomas and drew him aside and spoke three words to him.

When Thomas returned to his companions they asked him, "What did Jesus say to you?"

Thomas said to them, "If I tell you one of the words he spoke to me, you will pick up stones and throw them at me. And fire will come from the stones and burn you up."

Thomas is presented as the disciple most in awe of Jesus and the one favored with the secret knowledge.

Jesus said to them, "If you fast, you will 14
bring sin upon yourselves, and if you pray, you will
condemn yourselves, and if you give alms, you will
do evil to your spirits.

"When you enter any land and walk through its
regions, if they receive you, eat whatever they set
before you. Heal the sick among them. For that
which enters your mouth will not defile you, but
that which comes out of your mouth will defile
you."

When you see the one who was not born of 15
woman, fall on your faces and worship him. That
one is your father.

Similar to saying 11, this passage promises a heavenly vision, in
this case a being not born of woman.

16   People think it is peace I have come to
impose on the world, but they do not know it is
dissension I have come to cast on the earth: fire,
sword, war. For there will be five in a house: Three
will be against two and two against three, the
father against the son and the son against the
father, and they shall stand alone.

17   I shall give you what no eye has seen, what
no ear has heard and no hand has touched, and
what has not come into the human heart.

St. Paul also spoke of going beyond what can be seen and heard.
This image, widespread in antiquity, referred to visions and heavenly secrets.

THE DISCIPLES SAID TO JESUS, "Tell us how   18
our end will come."

Jesus said, "Have you discovered the beginning,
that you search for the end? In the place where
the beginning is, there the end will be. Blessed is he
who will stand at the beginning: He will know the
end and will not taste death."

BLESSED IS HE who existed before he was   19
created. If you become my disciples and hear my
words, these stones shall serve you. For there are
five trees in paradise that do not change in summer
or winter and whose leaves do not fall. Whoever
knows them shall not taste death.

Unlike the familiar quotes that surround it, this saying is Gnostic
in origin.

THE DISCIPLES SAID TO JESUS, "Tell us, what is the kingdom of heaven like?"

He said to them, "It is like a grain of mustard seed, smaller than all seeds. But when it falls on cultivated ground, it puts forth a large branch and provides a shelter for the birds of heaven."

For centuries, Jewish prophets compared the kingdom of heaven to the famed cedars of Lebanon, which were used to build the temple of Solomon in Jerusalem. So Jesus is shocking his audience by likening the kingdom to a tiny mustard seed, which grows into a scraggly plant most farmers considered a weed.

Mary said to Jesus, "What are your disciples like?"

He said, "They are like little children dwelling in a field that is not theirs. When the owners of the field come, they will say, 'Let us have our field back.' The disciples strip naked in front of the owners and give the field back to them.

"Therefore I say, if the owner of a house knows a thief is coming, he will stay awake and will not let the thief break into the house and carry away his goods.

"You must keep watch against the world. Arm yourselves with great power lest the robbers find a way to come upon you, because the difficulty you expect will materialize. Let there be a man of understanding among you.

"After the crop ripened, the owner came quickly with his sickle in his hand and reaped it. Whoever has ears to hear, let him hear."

In ancient culture, disciples and other followers were often referred to as "babes" or "children."

22　JESUS SAW SOME INFANTS being nursed and said to his disciples, "These children are like those who enter the kingdom."

They said to him, "If we are children shall we enter the kingdom?"

Jesus said to them, "When you make the two one, and when you make the inner like the outer and the outer like the inner, and the upper like the lower, and when you make the male and the female into a single one, so that the male is not male and the female not female, when you make eyes in place of an eye, a hand in place of a hand, a foot in place of a foot, and an image in place of an image, then you shall enter the kingdom."

According to Jewish wisdom literature, Adam was androgynous before the Fall. When men and women finally regain this earlier state of perfection, they will lose their sexual differences and become androgynous once more.

I WILL CHOOSE YOU, one from a thousand, and   23
two from ten thousand, and they will stand as a
single one.

His DISCIPLES SAID, "SHOW US the place   24
where you are, for we must seek it."

He said to them, "Whoever has ears to hear let
him hear. There is light within a man of light and it
illuminates the whole world. When it does not
shine, there is darkness."

If the line "He who has ears ... " sounds familiar, that's because it
also occurs in Matthew, Mark, Luke and even Revelation.

LOVE YOUR BROTHER like your soul; guard him   25
like the apple of your eye.

26   Y OU SEE THE SPLINTER in your brother's eye but you do not see the plank in your own eye. When you have taken the plank out of your own eye, then you will be able to see and remove the splinter from your brother's eye.

This famous sermon also appears in Matthew and Luke.

27   I F YOU DO NOT FAST with respect to the world, you will not find the kingdom. If you do not keep the sabbath as sabbath, you will not see the father.

Fasting from the world means giving up material things and pursuing a spiritual life.

I STOOD IN THE MIDST of the world and 28
appeared to them in the flesh. I found all of them
drunk, but I did not find any of them thirsty. My
soul ached for humanity's children because they are
blind in their hearts. They do not see that they
came empty into the world; and they seek to go
empty out of the world. Now they are drunk.
When they have shaken off their wine, then they
will repent.

Jesus speaks here as a heaven-sent redeemer, an image com-
monly used in the Gospel of John and among Gnostics.

IF THE FLESH EXISTS because of spirit, it is a 29
miracle; but if spirit exists because of the body, it
is a miracle of miracles. I marvel at how such great
wealth established itself amid this poverty.

Jesus seems almost bewildered at how a state as pure as the
spirit could be linked to something as mundane as the flesh.

30   Wʜᴇʀᴇ ᴛʜᴇʀᴇ ᴀʀᴇ ᴛʜʀᴇᴇ ɢᴏᴅs, they are gods. Where there are two or one, I am with him.

31   Nᴏ ᴘʀᴏᴘʜᴇᴛ ɪs ᴀᴄᴄᴇᴘᴛᴀʙʟᴇ in his own village; a physician does not heal those who know him.

This saying and the three that follow also appear in the New Testament gospels. Conservative scholars believe *Thomas* was dependent on Mark, Matthew and Luke whereas liberal historians contend it was written independently.

32   A ᴄɪᴛʏ built on a high mountain and well-fortified cannot fall, nor can it remain hidden.

WHAT YOU HEAR with your ear, preach in 33
others' ears from your housetops. For no one lights
a lamp and puts it under a bushel, nor does he put
it in a hidden place. Instead, he sets it on a
lampstand so that everyone who comes in and out
can see its light.

Lamps in the time of Jesus were small terra-cotta lanterns that
burned oil and were often the only source of light inside the
windowless houses of the region.

IF A BLIND MAN leads a blind man, both of 34
them will fall into a ditch.

IT IS IMPOSSIBLE FOR ANYONE to enter the 35
house of a strong man and take it by force without
first binding his hands. Then one will be able to
pillage the strong man's house.

36   Do not be anxious, from morning to evening and from evening to morning, about what you will wear.

37   His disciples asked, "When will you be revealed to us and when will we see you?"

Jesus said, "When you undress without being ashamed, and take your clothes and put them under your feet the way little children do and trample on them, then you will see the son of the living one and you will not be afraid."

Some scholars believe that the undressing mentioned here relates to the ceremony of baptism.

38   Many times you have desired to hear these words I speak to you, and you have had no one else from whom to hear them. The days will come when you will seek me and you will not find me.

THE PHARISEES AND THE SCRIBES have
received the keys of knowledge and have hidden
them. They did not enter and they did not allow
those who wanted to enter to do so. But you
should be wise as serpents and innocent as doves.

A VINE WAS PLANTED without the father, but
because it did not become strong it will be
uprooted and will rot.

HE WHO HAS SOMETHING in his hand will
receive more; and he who has nothing, even the
little he has will be taken away from him.

42 Bᴇᴄᴏᴍᴇ ᴘᴀꜱꜱᴇʀꜱʙʏ.

Another possible translation is "become wanderers," referring to the itinerant lifestyle of Jesus and his disciples.

43 Hɪꜱ ᴅɪꜱᴄɪᴘʟᴇꜱ ꜱᴀɪᴅ ᴛᴏ ʜɪᴍ, "Who are you that you should say these things to us?"

"In spite of what I say to you, you do not know who I am. You have become like the Jews: They love the tree but hate its fruit; they love the fruit but hate the tree."

44 Wʜᴏᴇᴠᴇʀ ʙʟᴀꜱᴘʜᴇᴍᴇꜱ against the father will be forgiven, and whoever blasphemes against the son will be forgiven, but whoever blasphemes against the holy spirit will not be forgiven, either on earth or in heaven.

GRAPES ARE NOT GATHERED from thorns nor 45
figs from thistles; they do not give fruit. A good
person brings forth good from his treasure; a bad
person brings forth evil from the evil treasure in his
heart, and he speaks evil. For out of the abundance
of his heart, he produces evil.

Sayings collections like *Thomas* grew out of the wisdom literature of the Middle East, which contained proverbs that presented simple truths about the individual and the world.

FROM ADAM TO JOHN the Baptist, among 46
those born of women no one is greater than John
the Baptist. But I said that anyone among you who
becomes as a child will know the kingdom and will
be superior to John.

47   Iᴛ ɪs ɪᴍᴘᴏssɪʙʟᴇ for a man to mount two horses or draw two bows. A servant cannot serve two masters; he will honor the one and scorn the other. No one drinks vintage wine and immediately wants to drink new wine. New wine is not put into old wine skins, for they might burst; and vintage wine is not poured into new wine skins, because it might spoil. No one sews an old patch on to a new garment, for it will tear.

48   Iꜰ ᴛᴡᴏ ᴍᴀᴋᴇ ᴘᴇᴀᴄᴇ with one another in the same house, they will say to the mountain, "Be moved!" and it will be moved.

49   Bʟᴇssᴇᴅ ᴀʀᴇ ᴛʜᴇ sᴏʟɪᴛᴀʀʏ and the chosen, for you will find the kingdom. Because you have come from it, you will go there again.

IF THEY SAY TO YOU, "Where did you come   50
from?" say to them, "We have come from the light,
the place where the light came into existence of
its own accord and revealed itself in their image." If
they say to you, "Who are you?" say to them, "We
are his sons and we are the chosen of the living
father." If they ask you, "What is the sign of your
father who is in you?" say to them, "It is a
movement and a repose."'

The questioners might be referring to the heavenly powers that
guard the passages back to the light, images often used in gnostic texts.

HIS DISCIPLES SAID TO HIM, "On what day will   51
the repose of the dead occur and when does the
new world come?"

He said to them, "That repose you look for has
come, but you have not recognized it."

52   HIS DISCIPLES SAID TO HIM, "Twenty-four prophets spoke in Israel and all of them spoke of you."

He said to them, "You have neglected the Living One in your presence and have spoken only about the dead."

53   HIS DISCIPLES SAID TO HIM, "Is circumcision worthwhile or not?"

He said to them, "If it were worthwhile, their father would beget them already circumcised from their mother. Rather, true circumcision in the spirit has become completely useful."

In the New Testament, St. Paul is portrayed as the first Christian to oppose the circumcision of Gentiles, but here Jesus himself is criticizing the custom.

54   BLESSED ARE THE POOR for yours is the kingdom of heaven.

H E WHO DOES NOT HATE his father and his   55
mother cannot be my disciple, and he who does
not hate his brothers and his sisters and does not
take up his cross as I have will not be worthy of me.

A strong element of social radicalism pervades Jesus' sayings,
even to the point of rejecting family.

H E WHO HAS COME to understand the world   56
has found a corpse; and the world is not worthy of
him who has found a corpse.

The expression "of him who has found a corpse" was used in
Jewish literature to praise someone.

57 THE KINGDOM OF THE FATHER is like a man who had good seed. His enemy came by night and sowed weeds among the good seed. But the man did not let anyone pull up the weed. He said, "Do not do so because when you go to pull up the weed you pull up the wheat along with it." On the day of the harvest the weeds will be conspicuous; they will be pulled up and burned.

The "weed" referred to may be a toxic plant called darnel that plagues wheat fields in the Middle East.

58 BLESSED IS THE MAN who has labored; he has found life.

59 LOOK UPON THE LIVING ONE as long as you live, lest you die and seek to see him but cannot see.

THEY SAW A SAMARITAN carrying a lamb as he   60
was going to Judea. He said to his disciples, "Why
does he carry the lamb?"

They said to him, "That he may kill it and eat
it."

He said to them, "As long as it is alive he will
not eat it; only if he has killed it and it has become
a corpse."

They said, "Otherwise he cannot eat it."

He said to them, "You yourselves must seek a
place for repose, or you might become corpses and
be eaten."

61 J ESUS SAID, "Two will be resting on a couch; one will die, the other will live."

Salome said, "Who are you, man? You have mounted my bed and have eaten from my table."

Jesus said to her, "I am the one who derives his being from the one who is undifferentiated. The things of my father have been given to me."

Salome said, "I am your disciple."

Jesus said to her, "Therefore, I say, whoever is united will be filled with light, but whoever is divided will be filled with darkness."

Salome is not being suggestive here: dinner guests in the early Mediterranean world normally reclined on couches placed near the table. Also of interest is that Salome, *a woman*, calls herself a disciple of Jesus.

62 I TELL MY MYSTERIES to those who are worthy of my mysteries. Do not let your left hand know what your right hand is doing.

THERE WAS A RICH MAN who had 63
considerable wealth. He said, "I will use my money
to sew and reap and plant and fill my warehouses
with fruit so that I will lack nothing." Such were his
intentions, but that night he died. Whoever has
ears, let him hear.

The tenuous nature of life is a vital theme in *Thomas* and
throughout Jesus' teachings.

A MAN HAD THE HABIT of receiving visitors. 64
When he had prepared a banquet he sent his
servant to invite the guests. The servant went to
the first and said to him, "My master invites you."

The man replied, "Money is owed me by some
merchants. They will come to me this evening; I
must go and give them orders. I beg to be excused
from the dinner."

The servant went to another and said to him,
"My master has invited you."

The second man said to him, "I have just bought
a house and am needed for a day. I have no time."

The servant went to another and said to him, "My master invites you."

That man said, "My friend is about to be married and I have to prepare a wedding feast; I will not be able to come. I beg to be excused from the dinner."

The servant went to another and said to him, "My master invites you."

He said to the servant, "I have bought a village and am on my way to collect the rent. I will not be able to come. I beg to be excused from the dinner."

The servant returned and said to his master, "Those you invited asked to be excused from the dinner."

The master said to his servant, "Go out into the streets and bring in those whom you find so that they may dine."

Buyers and merchants will not enter the places of my father.

This parable also appears in Matthew and Luke, where it is told differently, with embellishments that are political in nature. This has led some scholars to claim that the version in *Thomas* is closest to the actual story told by Jesus.

A GOOD MAN had a vineyard. He leased it to 65
some farmers so that they would cultivate it and
he would receive the fruit from them. He sent his
servant so that the tenants would give him the
fruit of the vineyard. They seized his servant, beat
him and almost killed him. The servant returned
and told his master. His master said, "Perhaps they
did not recognize him." He sent another servant.
The tenants beat him also. Then the master sent
his son. He said, "Perhaps they will respect my son."
The tenants, knowing he was the heir to the
vineyard, seized the son and killed him. Whoever
has ears, let him hear.

SHOW ME THE STONE that the builders 66
rejected. That is the cornerstone.

In early Christian imagery, the "rejected stone" is symbolic of
Jesus.

67   H<small>E</small> <small>WHO KNOWS ALL</small> but fails to know himself lacks everything.

68   B<small>LESSED ARE YOU</small> when you are hated and persecuted, and where you have been persecuted they will find no place.

This may refer to finding a place free from the Roman persecution of Christians and Jews in the first century A.D.

69   B<small>LESSED ARE THEY</small> who are persecuted in their heart; these are the ones who have truly known the father. Blessed are those who are hungry, for the belly of the needy will be filled.

WHEN YOU BRING FORTH what is in you, what   70
you have will save you. That which you do not have
in you will kill you if you do not know it within you.

In other words, salvation comes when the spiritual life is fully developed.

I SHALL DESTROY THIS HOUSE and no one will   71
be able to build it again.

In the New Testament gospels, Jesus talks about destroying the
temple in Jerusalem.

A MAN SAID TO JESUS, "Tell my brothers to   72
divide my father's possessions with me."

He said to the man, "O man, who made me a
divider?" He turned to his disciples and said to
them, "I am not a divider, am I?"

One interpretation is that "divider" actually refers to a schis-
matic and that Jesus is denying he is a heretic.

73   THE HARVEST IS GREAT but the laborers are
few, so pray to the Lord to send laborers to the
harvest.

74   LORD, THERE ARE MANY standing around the
drinking trough, but there is nothing in the well.

75   MANY ARE STANDING at the door, but those
who are alone are the ones who will enter the
bridal chamber.

THE KINGDOM OF THE FATHER is like a 76
merchant who had goods and found a pearl. This
merchant was wise. He sold the goods and bought
the one pearl for himself. You also must seek the
enduring treasure that does not perish, where no
moth enters to eat and no worm destroys.

Countercultural in their wisdom, several parables in *Thomas* portray people discovering their true identities and immediately considering the material world irrelevant.

I AM THE LIGHT that is above everything, I am 77
all; all came forth from me and all has returned to
me. Split the wood and I am there. Lift up the
stone and you will find me there.

78   W<small>HY DID YOU COME OUT</small> to the country? Was it to see a reed shaken by the wind? Or to see a man clothed in fine garments like your kings and great ones? They are clothed with fine raiment and they do not know the truth.

The version of this remark that appears in the New Testament refers to John the Baptist; but here, mysteriously, John is not mentioned.

79   A<small> WOMAN IN THE CROWD</small> said to him, "Blessed are the womb that bore you and the breasts that fed you."

He said to her, "Blessed are those who have heard the word of the father and have truly kept it. For the days will come when you will say, 'Blessed is the womb that has not conceived and the breasts that have not given milk.'"

This is both a plea to focus on the message rather than the man and an assertion that the natural family is inferior to the spiritual family.

Whoever has known the world has found 80
the body; but of whoever has found the body, the
world is not worthy.

In Gnosticism the world is often equated with death, something
that the individual seeker must transcend.

Let him who has become rich become king, 81
and let him who has power renounce it.

Whoever is near me is near fire, but 82
whoever is far from me is far from the kingdom.

There is a very similar Greek proverb that begins, "Whoever is
near Zeus is near the thunderbolt."

83   THE IMAGES ARE MANIFEST to the man, but the light in them is hidden in the image of the father's light. He will be revealed himself, but his image is hidden by his light.

Because of the confusing messages in this saying and the two that follow, some scholars believe that all three were added to the original text of *Thomas* at a later time.

84   WHEN YOU SEE YOUR LIKENESS, you rejoice. But when you see images of you that came into being before you, which do not die and are not made manifest, how much will you bear?

Gnostics believed that each individual possesses a new "body" or "image" that can be realized by transcending one's physical body and achieving the heavenly realm, where the new body is waiting.

ADAM CAME INTO EXISTENCE from great 85
power and great wealth and yet was not worthy of
you. For had he been worthy, he would not have
tasted death.

THE FOXES HAVE THEIR DENS and the birds 86
have their nests, but the son of man has nowhere
to lay his head and rest.

"Son of Man" was a common Jewish expression referring to a
"person" or a "human being."

WRETCHED IS THE BODY that is dependent 87
on a body and wretched is the soul that is
dependent on them both.

The message here is that anyone tied to the material world is
misguided and spiritually deficient.

88   THE ANGELS AND THE PROPHETS will come to you and give you what is yours. You also give them what is in your hands and say to yourselves, "On which day will they come and take what is theirs?"

89   WHY DO YOU WASH the outside of the cup? Do you not know that he who made the inside is also the one who made the outside?

Another of *Thomas'* wisdom sayings, this reflects on the foolish nature of human behavior.

90   COME TO ME, for my yoke is easy and my lordship is gentle and you will find repose for yourselves.

One of the spiritual quests of the Jewish wisdom movement, still popular during the time of *Thomas*, was the search for a divine "rest."

THEY SAID TO HIM, "Tell us who you are so   91
that we may believe in you."

He said to them, "You examine the face of the
heavens and the earth, and yet do not know what
is in front of your face nor do you know how to
discern this present time."

SEEK AND YOU WILL FIND, yet those things   92
you asked me in former times I did not tell you;
now when I want to tell you about them, you do
not ask.

DO NOT GIVE WHAT IS HOLY to dogs, because   93
they will throw it on the dung heap. Do not throw
pearls to swine.

In addition to this example, there are more than seventy parallels between the New Testament and the *Gospel of Thomas*.

94 WHOEVER SEARCHES WILL FIND. It will be
opened to him.

95 IF YOU HAVE MONEY, do not lend it at
interest, but give to those from whom you will not
receive it back.

96 THE KINGDOM OF THE FATHER is like a woman
who took a little leaven, hid it in dough and made
it into large loaves. Whoever has ears, let him hear.

This saying is characteristic of "growth parables" like the famous
saying about the mustard seed that Jesus compares to the kingdom of God.

THE KINGDOM OF THE FATHER is like a woman   97
who was carrying a jar full of meal. While she was
walking on a long road, the handle of the jar broke;
the meal spilled out behind her on to the road. She
did not notice it; she was unaware of the accident.
When she came to her house, she put the jar down
and found it was empty.

This saying, unique in Christian literature, means perhaps that
the kingdom can slip away if people aren't careful.

THE KINGDOM OF THE FATHER is like someone   98
who wanted to kill a powerful man. He drew the
sword in his own house and thrust it into the wall
so that he would know if his hand would be strong
enough. Then he killed the powerful one.

Also unique to the *Gospel of Thomas*, this is a chilling description
of an assassin.

99   THE DISCIPLES SAID TO HIM, "Your brothers and your mother are standing outside."

He said to them, "Those here who do the will of my father are my brothers and mother; it is they who will enter the kingdom of my father.

100   THEY SHOWED JESUS a gold coin and said to him, "Caesar's men demand taxes from us."

He said to them, "Give to Caesar what belongs to Caesar; give to God what belongs to God, and give to me what is mine."

101   HE WHO DOES NOT HATE his father and his mother as I do will not be able to be my disciple; and he who does not love his father and his mother as I do will not be able to be my disciple.

The contradiction implicit in Jesus telling his disciples to hate *and* love their parents can be explained if the second set refers to the holy spirit.

Dᴀᴍɴ ᴛʜᴇ Pʜᴀʀɪsᴇᴇs, for they resemble a   102
dog lying in an oxen manger, for he neither eats nor
lets the oxen eat.

The image of the dog in the cattle manger is common to ancient
literature, even appearing in the fables of Aesop.

Bʟᴇssᴇᴅ ɪs ᴛʜᴇ ᴍᴀɴ who knows where the   103
robbers will enter so that he may rise and gather his
strength and arm himself before they invade.

Tʜᴇʏ sᴀɪᴅ ᴛᴏ ʜɪᴍ, "Come, let us pray today   104
and let us fast."

Jesus said, "Why? What sin have I committed or
how have I been conquered? After the bridegroom
has left the bridechamber, then let people fast and
pray."

105   Hᴇ ᴡʜᴏ ᴋɴᴏᴡꜱ father and mother will be called the son of a harlot.

106   Wʜᴇɴ ʏᴏᴜ ᴍᴀᴋᴇ ᴛʜᴇ ᴛᴡᴏ ᴏɴᴇ, you shall become sons of man, and when you say, "Mountain, be moved!" it will move.

Like saying 22, the two becoming one refers to men and women returning to the androgynous state enjoyed by Adam before the fall.

107   Tʜᴇ ᴋɪɴɢᴅᴏᴍ is like a shepherd who had a hundred sheep. One of them, the largest, went astray. The shepherd left the ninety-nine and searched for that one until he found it. After he had labored he said to the sheep, "I love you more than the ninety-nine."

It was a rare lamb that was lost in first-century Israel. Each shepherd had a unique whistle known only to his flock. If two flocks became hopelessly intermixed at a watering spot, the herder needed simply to whistle softly for his flock to immediately part from the other sheep and follow him.

WHOEVER DRINKS from my mouth will be as I   108
am, and I shall be that person, and the hidden
things will be revealed to that person.

THE KINGDOM is like a man who had a treasure   109
hidden in his field without knowing of it. After he
died he left the field to his son, who also did not
know. The son who inherited the field sold it. The
one who bought the field found the treasure while
he was plowing. He began to lend money at
interest to whomever he wished.

This image of wisdom as hidden treasure occurs in Proverbs,
Matthew and also in Aesop's Fables.

LET HIM WHO HAS FOUND the world and   110
become rich deny the world.

111 THE HEAVENS AND THE EARTH will be rolled up in your presence and he who lives in the living one will not see death.

Does not Jesus say, "He who finds himself, of him the world is not worthy?"

Like the preceding saying, this carries a countercultural message that runs through *Thomas*—worldly values are spiritually insufficient and should be rejected.

112 WOE TO THE FLESH that depends on the soul; woe to the soul that depends on the flesh.

113 HIS DISCIPLES SAID TO HIM, "When will the kingdom come?"

He said, "It will not come when it is expected. They will not say, 'Look here,' or 'Look there.' Rather the kingdom of the father is spread out on the earth and people do not see it."

Simon Peter said to them, "Let Mary leave us, because women are not worthy of life."

Jesus said, "Look, I shall lead her so that I can make her male in order that she also may become a living spirit resembling you males. For every woman who makes herself male will enter the kingdom of heaven."

Peter, who is the most important disciple in the New Testament, has much lower status in *The Gospel of Thomas*. Mary, on the other hand, is elevated to a special place.

The Gospel according to Thomas

The last line of the text attributes the gospel to Thomas, whereas the introductory line refers to Didymos Judas Thomas. "Thomas" is the Semitic expression for "twin" and "Didymos" means the same thing in Greek; only Judas is a real name. This has led some scholars to contend that the author really being credited was Judas, the brother of Jesus. Regardless of whether the official author was Jesus' brother or "doubting Thomas," it has never been determined that either person was involved with *The Gospel of Thomas*.

PART THREE

Paradise Regained: A Commentary

by John Dominic Crossan

THE GOSPEL OF THOMAS BEGINS BY ANNOUNCING
that it contains *secret* sayings from Jesus. Since these utterances have been written down for anyone to read, however, their secrecy is not a matter of physical concealment
but of concealed meaning. What, then, is the hidden message of this gospel? What is the secret Jesus claims could
protect one from tasting death and ensure eternal life?

Even a cursory glance through the gospel reveals a
profound distaste for anything related to the worldly life.
Jesus comes with fire and sword, lashing out at a place full
of blind, drunk inhabitants. He tells his disciples to guard
against, fast from, and renounce that world—its ways are
as empty as a carcass:

> He who has come to understand the world has found
> a corpse; and the world is not worthy of him who has
> found a corpse. (Saying 56)

If you are radically disenchanted with some place, you
can go, presumably, to another present location and find a

better world. You can go, at least in imagination, beneath the earth, beyond the seas or above the stars, to discover somewhere a perfect utopia. But, if the whole world seems truly corrupt, empty and dead, your only option may be to travel in time—forward to the future or back into the past. For a more fulfilling life, seek the beginning or the end, Eden or Apocalypse.

The Q Gospel, a text now embedded in the gospels of Matthew and Luke, looks forward to the end, imagining a perfect world after all else is complete. But the *Gospel of Thomas* chooses the opposite path. It goes backwards to a perfect beginning, not to apocalypse consummated but to paradise regained. Alienated within the world's present normalcy, it proposes a way to the dawn of creation.

The first step on this backward journey shows Jesus as the incarnation of divine wisdom, admonishing a lost world to change its ways. This appeal not only emphasizes how perfect the created universe had originally been, it ridicules any yearning for a terminal solution. The Jesus of this Gospel knows all about alternatives that look forward to the End, and insists we avoid such misguided prospects. The theology he presents is not Eden *and* Apocalypse or Eden *without* Apocalypse but Eden *against* Apocalypse. When the disciples look ahead to the future consummation, Jesus tells them they have missed the new world already dawning in their midst. The ideal kingdom is not in the future.

Jesus jeers at the idea of an apocalyptic kingdom appearing from the heavens—if it does, he says, the birds will get into it first. Or maybe it will appear in the sea and the fishes will get in first. Don't be deceived, insists Jesus —the kingdom is already with us. The first step back, therefore, is to see the absurdity of looking to the future.

The second step, more positive than the first, sends us back to reclaim the Garden of Eden—not only before original sin destroyed its perfection but even earlier, before the split into male and female made that sin possible. As this gospel interprets Genesis 1-3, Adam is not just Adam-the-Male as distinct from Eve-the-Female, but rather Adam-the-Human, a being neither male nor female —or, if you prefer, both male and female. Before Adam was split into male and female beings, the heavenly archetype and earthly manifestation of "Adam" were androgynous. That neither-male-nor-female state, says Jesus, is what we must reclaim, a challenge asserted most clearly in this well-known saying:

> Jesus saw some infants being nursed and said to his disciples, "These children are like those who enter the kingdom." They said to him, "If we are children shall we enter the kingdom?" Jesus said to them, "When you make the two one, and when you make the inner like the outer and the outer like the inner, and the upper like the lower, and when you make the male and the female into a single one, so that the

male is not male and the female not female, when
you make eyes in place of an eye, a hand in place of a
hand, a foot in place of a foot, and an image in place
of an image, then you shall enter the kingdom."
(Saying 22)

The newborn child's asexual nature becomes a perfect model for the unified state Jesus says we must aspire
to. Outer physical differences must become like inner
spiritual similarities. The upper heavenly archetype must
correspond precisely with the lower earthly reality. In this
ideal formulation, by the way, male and female are equal.
Neither sex existed prior to the original separation that
created both at the same time.

The third step is the most fundamental. How, in actual practice, do you get back to that unified state presented in the Eden of Genesis 1–3? The answer, and the
secret's deepest core, is through celibate asceticism. That is
how you reclaim Paradise Lost, how you make the male
and the female into a single one, how you become "soli-
tary" or "alone" as in sayings 15, 49 and 75. It is also why
so many of the standard modes of piety are no longer ad-
equate. They all pale into triviality compared with the
radical world-negation demanded by ascetic celibacy.

His disciples asked him, "Do you want us to fast?
How shall we pray? Shall we give alms? What diet
shall we keep?" (Saying 6)

Jesus said to them, "If you fast, you will bring sin upon yourselves, and if you pray, you will condemn yourselves, and if you give alms, you will do evil to your spirits." (Saying 14)

These ordinary modes would only lull you into a false sense of security. Instead you must give up the world entirely:

If you do not fast with respect to the world, you will not find the kingdom. If you do not keep the sabbath as sabbath, you will not see the father. (Saying 27)

Let him who has found the world and become rich deny the world. (Saying 110)

One must fast from the normalcy of the world itself. One must observe not just a weekly Sabbath, but that original rest as God observed it at the dawn of creation. One must give not just alms, but whatever is demanded.

This, in swiftest summary, is the secret teaching of *The Gospel of Thomas*. Return to the primordial moment of creation. Go back before the Fall, before the original Sin that made the Fall inevitable, and, above all, before the split that made sin and Fall possible. The ideal state proclaimed by *The Gospel of Thomas* is that of the primordial human being, a single and unified Adam, neither male nor female. One returns to this state by asceticism, by celibacy, by leaving any worldly life behind.

Become passersby. (Saying 42)

Bibliography

Attridge, Harold W. "The Gospel of Thomas." In *Harper's Bible Dictionary*, edited by Paul J. Achtemeier. San Francisco: Harper & Row, 1985.

Biblical Archeologist, Fall 1979. The issue is devoted entirely to the Nag Hammadi discovery, including two fact-filled articles by Robinson.

Borg, Marcus, ed. *The Lost Gospel Q: The Original Sayings of Jesus*. Berkeley: Ulysses Press, 1996.

Ceram, C.W. *Gods, Graves, and Scholars*. Rev. ed. New York: Alfred A. Knopf, [1951] 1967.

Dart, John. *The Jesus of Heresy and History: The Discovery and Meaning of the Nag Hammadi Gnostic Library*. San Francisco: Harper & Row, 1988.

Davies, Stevan L. *The Gospel of Thomas and Christian Wisdom*. New York: Seabury Press, 1983.

Doresse, Jean. "A Gnostic Library from Upper Egypt." *Archeology* (Summer 1950).

_____. *The Secret Books of the Egyptian Gnostics: An Introduction to the Gnostic Coptic Manuscripts Discovered at Chenoboskion*. New York: Viking, 1960. Doresse's story of the discovery and his translation of *The Gospel of Thomas*.

Funk, Robert, Roy W. Hoover, and the Jesus Seminar. (cq) *The Five Gospels: The Search for the Authentic Words of Jesus*. New York: Macmillan Publishing Co., 1993.

Gaertner, Bertil. *The Theology of the Gospel According to Thomas*. New York: Harper & Row, 1961.

Guillaumont, A., H.-Ch. Puech, G. Quispel, W. Till, and Yassah 'Abd Al Masih. *The Gospel According to Thomas*. Leiden: E. J. Brill; New York: Harper & Row, 1959.

Kloppenborg, John S., Marvin W. Meyer, Stephen J. Patterson, Michael G. Steinhauser. *Q Thomas Reader*. Sonoma: Polebridge Press, 1990.

Koester, Helmut. *Introduction to the New Testament, vol. 2, History and Literature of Early Christianity*. Philadelphia: Fortress, 1982.

_____. *Ancient Christian Gospels*. Philadelphia: Trinity Press International, 1990.

Lewis, Bernard. *The Middle East: A Brief History of the Last 2,000 Years*. New York: Touchstone, 1995.

Menard, Jacques E. "Thomas, Gospel of." In *The Interpreter's Dictionary of the Bible, Supplementary Volume*, edited by Keith Crum. Nashville: Abingdon, 1976.

Meyer, Marvin, tr. *The Gospel of Thomas: The Hidden Sayings of Jesus*. New York: HarperCollins Publishers, 1992.

Pagels, Elaine. *The Gnostic Gospels*. New York: Random House, 1979.

Patterson, Stephen J. *The Gospel of Thomas and Jesus*. Sonoma: Polebridge Press, 1993.

Pearson, Birger A. "Nag Hammadi Codices." In *1974 Yearbook of the Encyclopedia Judaica*. Jerusalem: Keter Publishing House, 1974.

Perrin, Norman. *Rediscovering the Teaching of Jesus*. New York: Harper & Row, 1967.

Richardson, Dan. *Egypt*. London: The Rough Guides, 1996.

Robinson, James M. *The Nag Hammadi Codices, a general introduction to the nature and significance of the Coptic Gnostic Library from Nag Hammadi*. 2nd rev. ed. Claremont: Institute for Antiquity and Christianity, 1977.

_____. "Nag Hammadi: The First Fifty Years." *Occasional Papers Number 34*. Claremont: Institute for Antiquity and Christianity, 1995.

_____. *The Nag Hammadi Library in English*. Third rev. ed., San Francisco: Harper & Row, 1988.

Yadin, Yigael. *The Message of the Scrolls*. New York: Simon and Schuster, 1957.

About the Authors

JOHN DART has covered religion news for the *Los Angeles Times* since 1967. He is author of *The Jesus of Heresy and History* and was on the board of the Society of Biblical Literature's Pacific Coast Region 1990–95. He is a former president of the Religion Newswriters Association. A second edition of his widely used *Deities & Deadlines, a Primer on Religion News Coverage*, was published in 1998.

RAY RIEGERT is an editor of *The Lost Gospel Q* and *Jesus and Buddha: The Parallel Sayings*. A member of the Society of Biblical Literature and the American Association of Religion, he has written for newspapers and magazines throughout the United States. Ray is also a travel writer with eight books to his credit, including *Hidden Hawaii*, currently in its tenth edition.

JOHN DOMINIC CROSSAN, a world-renowned expert on the historical Jesus, is the author of *The Birth of Christianity*, *Jesus: A Revolutionary Biography* and *The Historical Jesus*. He is a member of the Jesus Seminar.